W9-BEP-771

The Indoor Water Gardener's How-To Handbook

H. Peter Loewer
Illustrations by the author

WALKER AND COMPANY
New York

First published in the United States of America in 1973 by the Walker Publishing Company, Inc.

Published simultaneously in Canada by Fitzhenry & Whiteside, Limited, Toronto.

ISBN: 0-8027-0404-2

Library of Congress Catalog Card Number: LC 72-95755

Printed in the United States of America

10   9   8   7   6   5   4   3   2   1

CONTENTS

PREFACE   5
Chapter 1 • HYDROCULTURE AND WHY   9
Chapter 2 • GETTING STARTED   13
Chapter 3 • PLANTS FOR YOUR WATER
        GARDEN   22
Chapter 4 • BULBS AND WATER   77
Chapter 5 • ALL ABOUT CONTAINERS   87
Chapter 6 • SOURCES OF SUPPLY   94
INDEX   96

LIST OF PLANTS ILLUSTRATED

Page
Number   *In order of appearance in the text*

25   African Evergreen — *Syngonium podophyllum*
26   Arrowhead Plant — *Syngonium podophyllum
         'Atrovirens'*
       Trileaf Wonder — *Syngonium podophyllum
         'Trileaf Wonder'*
28   Bloodleaf — *Iresine herbstii*
       Yellow Bloodleaf — *Iresine lindenii formosa*
30   Pewter Chinese Evergreen — *Aglaonema
         commutatum 'Pewter'*
33   Painted Nettle — *Coleus blumei 'Brilliancy'*
35   Striped Dracaena — *Dracaena deremensis
         'Warneckei'*
37   Gold-dust Dracaena — *Dracaena godseffiana*
38   Madagascar Dragon Tree — *Dracaena marginata*

39   Ribbon Plant — *Dracaena sanderiana*
42   Golden Dumbcane — *Dieffenbachia picta 'Rudolph Roehrs'*
44   Manda's Crested Ivy — *Hedera helix 'Manda's Crested'*
       Hahn's Selfbranching Ivy — *Hedera helix 'Hahn's Selfbranching'*
45   Triton Ivy — *Hedera helix 'Triton'*
       English Ivy — *Hedera helix*
       Diamond Ivy — *Hedera helix 'Little Diamond'*
       Fluffy Ruffles Ivy — *Hedera helix 'Fluffy Ruffles'*
48   Hawaiian Ti — *Cordyline terminalis bicolor*
49   Hawaiian Tree Fern — *Cibotium chamissoi*
50   Japanese Spurge — *Pachysandra terminalis*
52   Miniature Sweet Flag — *Acorus gramineus variegatus*
54   Variegated Ivy Tree — *Fatshedera lizei variegata*
57   Burgundy Philodendron — *Philodendron × 'Burgundy'*
59   Heartleaf Philodendron — *Philodendron oxycardium (cordatum)*
60   Fiddle-leaf Philodendron (juvenile) — *Philodendron panduraeforme*
61   Cut-leaved Philodendron — *Philodendron radiatum (dubium)*
62   Silver-leaf Philodendron (juvenile form) — *Philodendron sodiroi*
63   Piggy-back Plant — *Tolmiea menziesii*
66   Satin Pothos — *Scindapsus pictus argyraeus*
71   Umbrella Plant — *Cyperus diffusus*
73   Umbrella Tree — *Brassaia actinophylla*
74   Variegated Wandering Jew — *Zebrina pendula 'Discolor'*
79   French Roman Hyacinth — *Hyacinthus orientalis*
82   Lily-of-the-Valley — *Convallaria majalis*
84   Yellow Crocus — *Crocus chrysanthus*
85   Soleil d'Or Narcissus — *Narcissus tazetta*

PREFACE

This book got its start ten years ago when my wife and I came from the green fields of a rural community in upstate New York to find all the "glitterings" that a big city has to offer. We settled in the Lower East Side of Manhattan, four flights up, in a small apartment with two windows facing an airshaft. Our front door was made of balsa wood and frosted glass reinforced with chicken wire, and there was not a piece of clover in sight.

After the first three months of a typical New York winter, we needed something to remind us of our country heritage and decided to buy a few house plants to brighten the environment. Dashing down to the local florist, we bought a Christmas pepper, a mother-in-law's-tongue (the florist, whom I remember as a fairly decent type, told us that "nothing on God's green earth can kill them!"), a rather limp philodendron, and an African violet.

Like most newly arrived New Yorkers, we spent most of our free time away from home, and the steam heat began to have its effect: the violet just turned brown and crinkled up, despite endless soakings in the sink. In fact, one evening, in darkness, I turned on the shower without seeing that all four of our green friends were soaking themselves in the tub where my wife had kindly placed them. (The bathroom light switch was inoperable; it was behind the door, which had to be left open to admit heat from the kitchen as the landlord had completely overlooked any source of warmth for the bathroom.) One blast from the shower and a great deal of soil went down the drain and up the walls.

After cleaning up, we went foraging for soil in Central Park where we filled several small paper bags which we smuggled home on the subway.

Soon the white flies and aphids arose from their winter slumber and proceeded literally to tear the pepper to shreds. Then in late March, the heat inside the apartment soared to 94°, even with the two windows and the hall door open. The plants were parched. Because the cold-water pipes had broken that afternoon and no one in the building had cold water, we put pans of hot water in the refrigerator to cool, but to no avail; the plants expired.

After we moved to our next apartment, I remembered my mother's garden and her endless plant cuttings, quietly rooting in water in jelly glasses on the back porch. Why not just grow them in water? There would be no pots, no dirt, and no daily watering. We wouldn't have to transform the bathroom or kitchen into a potting shed.

We started with a couple of ivy cuttings donated by a Long Island friend, and from then on, at first in the city, more recently in our house in the woods, our water garden has been growing and growing.

H.P.L.

An attractive centerpiece made from an old battery jar, clear glass marbles and cuttings of Umbrella Plant, Chinese Evergreen, Ribbon Plant, Gold-dust Dracaena, and Wandering Jew.

8

chapter 1 • HYDROCULTURE AND WHY

Q Hydroculture, or hydroponics (growing plants in
water), has a history of almost 300 years, from
the experiments by the English botanist John
Woodward, who was trying to discover how
plants received their nutrients from the soil,
to the giant, glass and plastic, fully automated,
factory greenhouses of the twentieth century
where vegetables, from watercress to tomatoes, are grown commercially by the ton.

On a more homey scale, the Sunday
supplements of the late thirties had many a
housewife believing that a small tank near her
kitchen would soon produce all the vegetables, fruits, and salads needed by a healthy,
modern family. By the forties, popular maga-
zine and newspaper articles predicted that
whole armies would be fed by plants grown
without soil in food factories that operated
twenty-four hours a day. Visions of giant zuc-
chinis danced in the heads of farmers and

9

grocers alike. Today's hydroponic speculations conjure up elaborate spaceship gardens that utilize the wastes of the crew for the necessary carbon dioxide and nutrients to produce extraterrestrial fruits and juicy algae.

For earthbound gardeners, the promise of hydroculture is more modest — and much closer at hand. The satisfactions of water gardening are available to anyone who likes a bit of greenery in the home all year round and who will spare five minutes a week for the care of a few plants. No doubt you have tried your hand with house plants. No doubt you have had some successes, but these successes, unless you have an uncommonly green thumb, have been mixed with frequent failures. And I'll wager that most of your failures can be attributed to one single problem: *improper watering.*

Before I took up hydroculture, I found I invariably missed one of my house plants on my watering rounds. I thought I had everything down to a perfect schedule: plant X gets water once a week only in the summer (except on rainy days) and in the winter when the leaves begin to droop, plant Y gets water twice a day, and plant Z on the first day of spring. Suddenly I'd be called out of town for a few days and return to find not only X, but Y and Z as well, in small heaps on desiccated soil.

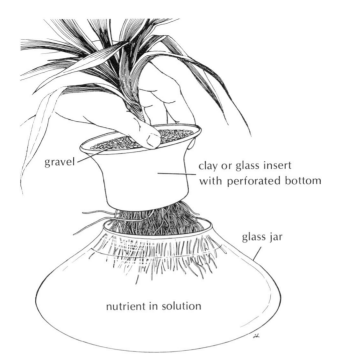

gravel

clay or glass insert
with perforated bottom

glass jar

nutrient in solution

With water gardening, I just make sure all vessels are full before leaving and return in a week, or even two, to find all leaves lush and green.

Not only does hydroculture substantially increase your win-loss score as an indoor gardener, but it will make you a wizard decorator as well. The decorative possibilities of the plants and their root systems, which form fantastic patterns in the glassware, are endless. If you need a unique centerpiece for that projected dinner party, just go to your water garden a few minutes before the guests arrive and remove two or three plants of pleasing colors and textures, wash them, roots and all, combine them in an attractive jar, add a few glass marbles or pebbles for support—and water—and you have it made—without a costly trip to the florist.

In Europe, hydroculture is already a busy and booming hobby. Special pots and vessels are available at most garden centers. Premeasured nutrient solutions come in pill form, along with instructions so detailed that success is guaranteed. Pots are usually in two sections: an outer jar of glass or ceramic glazed on both inner and outer surfaces to protect the finish of expensive furniture, and an inner pot (unglazed) with a perforated bottom to hold the plants.

In this country, where such information and equipment are not generally available, we'll launch you on a water-gardening career that is relatively inexpensive, carefree, and creative. Furthermore, we can guarantee that you will have no soil-borne pests and diseases, and no problems of what to do with that half bushel of dank soil in the sink. Although we can't offer a crop of ten-pound melons and quarts of beautiful red tomatoes, we can help you fill that empty counter in front of the north window—finally—with a picture of green that will be a delight for months, even years.

chapter 2 • GETTING STARTED

I've already said water gardening is simple, so I shall not dwell on rules and instructions. Here is a quick list of things you will need and a few basic tricks of the trade:

Containers: Any vessel that will hold water will serve—except for copper, brass, or lead containers which will generate harmful chemicals as they interact with water and plant food.

There is a whole chapter on finding and making containers toward the end of the book (see page 87); here I will have my say about clear versus colored glass. The main objection to clear glass in hydroculture is that, with a strong light source and extra nutrients, a large quantity of algae will soon grow up. The darker the glass, the fewer the algae; in an opaque container there will be none.

Despite this argument, I'm a clear-glass

advocate myself. As I've never had more than 30 or 40 containers in use at once, and, as replacement materials are, to say the least, inexpensive, I find the routine of changing waters, rinsing the roots, and re-shaping my plants, once every month or so, a very relaxing way to spend an evening.

The best argument for clear glass is that I find the root development of my water plants just as fascinating to watch as the growth of greenery on top. Some authorities claim that sunlight damages roots, but I don't believe it (unless they are left totally unprotected in a hot summer sun so that the water virtually boils them to death). Choice of glass, of course, is entirely up to you.

Stones and Gravels: In the right containers, many plants need no support other than the sides of the vessel itself. Many other plants may need support at first, but soon their roots will fill the container and provide a firm base.

When my water-grown plants need support, or a "holdfast," I've always used aquarium gravel purchased at the pet counter at variety stores. Beach pebbles are grand looking, but make sure that they are absolutely clean of ocean salt, even if you have found them yards above the high-tide line. Beach sand, while sparkly and attractive, is just too heavily laced with salt ever to be sufficiently rinsed clean in the kitchen sink. Marble chips eventually change the pH of the water, so I've been told, so their use is, or would be, an experiment. Bricks, when broken into small pieces, are usable. Clear glass marbles make beautiful holdfasts; being a purist, I dislike the colored varieties.

Bottle Brushes: These are a necessity, as you will appreciate if you've ever tried to clean many containers with rolled-up paper towels. If you have none on hand, bottle brushes are available at chemical supply outlets (see Chapter 6) and at most hardware stores.

Misting Can: Many rooms today tend to be overheated and therefore very dry, so that a daily spraying with a mist of warm water is essential for plants that like higher humidity.

Watering Can: Preferably, your watering can should have a long spout. It will allow you to reach containers in the back row and to pour accurately, thus avoiding spills.

Water: Your water supply is not overwhelmingly critical. Many indoor water gardeners get good results with tap water (so long as it is not icy cold).

For best results, however, you must keep an eye on the acidity and chlorine levels of your water. You should have a simple pH measuring tape which is available from most garden centers or by mail through the larger seed catalogues; the pH tape is used for testing the acid or alkaline content of water. Most municipal waters in the eastern United States tend to be alkaline because of the limestone in the rock of surrounding watersheds. The scale runs from pH 3 (very acid) to pH 7 (neutral) and on up to pH 9 (very alkaline).

Most plants prefer water between pH 6 and pH 7. If your water is too alkaline, collect a gallon in a clean vessel and add a few drops of vinegar. Test again. When you arrive at the right mixture, make a note of it for future reference. If the water is too acid (which is unlikely), add a few drops of a solution of bicarbonate of soda. I might add that I have found the pH rating to be critical only with the Umbrella Plants.

The greatest danger in municipal water is chlorine. It will work its way out of standing water in a day or two. If your family can do without the bathtub for a while, run water into it to a depth of about 3 inches and let it sit for thirty-six hours. (No other container in the house has so large a surface area.)

Another method is to keep a large crock of water on hand so that you always have a couple of gallons of chlorine-free water ready to use.

Don't use water softened by a home appliance. Water softeners work by means of an exchange of chemicals; the result may be pleasant to bathe in, but the plants do not enjoy it.

Rain water and snow are excellent, although if collected in heavily urban areas they will have absorbed chemicals and particles while falling through the air. I must confess that, when living in the city, I used city rain water all the time with no adverse effects. Of course use fresh, clean rain water and newly fallen snow. With snow, remember that it takes several shovels full to make an adequate supply of water.

Plant Food: Most garden books and house-plant manuals give recipes for making one's own plant food. It's not hard to do, but it does require shopping around to find the chemicals needed and then you must have a place to store them.

Another way is to buy one of the commercially prepared soluble powders found now even in most supermarkets. For our purposes, any of them are acceptable except for one variety that turns the solution blue (unless you like blue water).

Mix a gallon or more ahead of time according to the instructions on the powder container so that a mixed supply is always on hand. A good rule: Cut the powder instructions by half. It is far better to underfeed than overfeed. Remember that most of the plants that I list don't need food to survive, but with food they all will grow a bit faster. This becomes the "nutrient solution" that I mention below.

Notebook: It's always a good idea to keep a record of the day the plants are received; where a particular plant came from; when you have decided to increase or decrease the use of the nutrient solution; whether a plant does better in one light source or another; the effects of different temperatures; and so on. You always think you'll remember because it seemed so important at the time, but the memory soon fades, so that you may have to begin that particular experiment over again.

First Steps: If your new plant is a cutting, it is ready for the water. If your new plant comes in a pot with soil, turn it over and, holding the plant stem and dirt with one hand, knock the pot on the edge of a table. Unless the soil is very wet, a clump of earth surrounding the roots will loosen and fall out. Plastic pots can be cut with scissors and removed in pieces.

Then take the ball of earth and place it in a clean pan of tepid water; let it soak until the earth falls away from the roots. Do this a second time until the roots are quite clean, being very careful so as to prevent unnecessary destruction. Now rinse the roots under a gentle flow of tepid water. Next, take a container and put a few small pieces of charcoal in the bottom, then add the plant and enough plain water to cover the roots and part of the stem. Never let any leaves remain under the water surface as they will rot. *Don't forget the charcoal;* it is important because it will keep the water clear and pure. If you have a wood-burning fireplace, you have ample charcoal on hand. Otherwise, you can purchase it at variety or pet stores.

The above procedure is fine for Chinese Evergreens, Ivies, Dracaenas, cuttings, and the like. But if the plant is to stand alone in the container, such as Umbrella Plants or Tree Ferns, you will want to spread the roots gently in well-rinsed gravel or stones.

After a few days, replace the plain water (if the plant calls for it) with your already prepared nutrient solution. As the water evaporates, add more plain water to the desired level. Never add nutrient solution to replace evaporated water because, each time you do, the concentration of chemicals will become stronger.

You will soon see new white roots beginning to form, and, as the plant becomes acclimatized, top growth will be evident.

Changing Water: If the plants are doing well, don't bother to change the water unless you have an unpleasant accumulation of algae or some dead roots that should be removed. At least once a month, however, change your solutions, because the plant roots do need oxygen from the air or fresh water. Although a container with a large surface area will allow a certain amount of oxygen to enter the water by diffusion, and the fresh water you add will contain oxygen, it's always a good idea to have a complete change. European water gardeners often use bicycle pumps or aquarium aereators to pump oxygen bubbles through the solutions every few days.

Remember that water changing is an area wide open to experimentation. Suppose that one of the plants does not respond very well. Check your light requirements, your temperature, and your nutrient solutions. When experimenting with nutrients, always *dilute* your basic mixtures. More does not mean better; it often means final destruction, as too much of these chemicals can kill any plants.

Cleaning of dust and pests: In the most well-ordered home, everything gets dusty, and plant leaves are no exception. Dust on leaves does nothing to help the plant, as it cuts down on light.

Use a camel's hair brush for occasional brush-offs, and soap and water if the leaves of any plant become layered with grime, which can easily happen in most cities these days. In cleaning your plants, don't be afraid to use a mild solution of soap and tepid water. It won't hurt the plant as long as everything is finally rinsed with clean water. Don't use cold water.

If you provide regular leaf brushing, say once every two weeks, you should have no pest problems. You may bring in some insects with a new plant from a store, and the best solution is to quarantine new arrivals for a week or so to see if any pests appear.

The only insects you are likely to have are white flies and spider mites. Both are easy enough to find if you examine your plants closely. White flies are tiny white insects that flutter about when leaves are disturbed. They lay their eggs, and exist chiefly, on the under sides of leaves, and they will in time destroy the plant. Two kinds of spider mites are found on plants in the home; the Ivies particularly attract them. It doesn't make a whit of difference which kind of spider mite you get; they are all bad. They spin tiny webs and live under the leaves, eventually killing the plant. Washing the leaves with soap and water will vanquish them. If for some reason you cannot eliminate them, use a chemical spray (Malathion) but only as a last resort.

chapter 3 · PLANTS FOR YOUR WATER GARDEN

The following is an informal description of plants that I have tried in my home and found suitable for hydroculture, and have grown with a minimum of fuss. There are, I'm sure, many, many more, and most plants will respond to hydroponic care when properly potted and supervised. Even some cacti do well in water. For our present purposes, however, we are concerned with those plants that will do well in plain water or a mild nutrient solution, that require no specialized environments or intricate routines of care, and that will adapt to interesting and decorative containers which can be readily moved around a busy home.

I list the plants alphabetically by common name, followed by the Latin name, and give brief descriptions. At the top right of each entry, you will find temperature and light information, as, for example, "warm/partial shade" or "cool/sun." All these terms are defined below.

Temperature: *Cool* means 40° to 50° F.; *moderately warm* ranges from 55° to 65° F.; and *warm* refers to 65° to 70° F.

Note that these temperatures refer to *nighttime* only. Most plants require a drop in temperature at night for healthy growth. In the warm houses and apartments of today, you can usually provide for a temperature drop by placing plants close to a window at night.

Average indoor *daytime* temperatures which may go well above 70° F. should not adversely affect any of the plants listed in this book.

As for the lower range, if you turn the heat down when you go away on a trip, your water plants will do well for a week or two as long as the temperature doesn't go below 50°. If you plan to leave your house cool, move your most sensitive plants away from window locations.

Light: *Sun* means a south window, or at least four hours of sun a day; *partial shade*, an east or west window; and *shade*, a north window.

Descriptions: An informal description of each genus and of each individual species, with the botanical names in Latin, are given. When ordering plants, you should always use the botanical, or Latin, name because many plants have common names that are different in one region from those in another, but there is only one scientific name, which is the one in Latin. Generally speaking, catalogues list plants by the Latin names to avoid confusion.

An *asterisk* indicates that the plant is illustrated; I've illustrated only those plants that are in my collection. Each is drawn from life, an experience that has helped me to provide some shadings and textures that are not usually available. I show each plant in a different kind of container as a means of suggesting the virtually infinite variety that you can find or make.

Arrowheads, *Syngonium*

Warm/Partial shade

Creeping or climbing vines with shiny leaves generally shaped like arrowheads, which seem to thrive even when tossed into an old Mason jar and left for weeks in a dark corner. They're excellent plants for the coffee table or bookshelf, but they like a bright shaded area in the summertime. When they begin to climb, I generally use nylon fishing line for a support, one end tied to a stone and placed in the container and the other end tacked to the window frame or wall. You'll find them for sale in most dime stores, and florists have used them in dish gardens for

are cautioned therefore to keep the plants well out of the reach of children.

   D. amoena: Giant Dumbcane. A very large and handsome plant with glossy, oblong, pointed leaves, deep green and covered with yellowish white bands and splotches. A gardener friend had this plant in her living room. When it reached the ceiling, it made a right-angle turn and proceeded to grow horizontally until the weight cracked the cane at about the 5-foot level. A durable plant!

D. picta 'Rudolph Roehrs': Golden Dumbcane. Leaves are a yellowish green, with creamy-white splotches. My one success; the plant is in an upstairs room of continual warmth. A west window gives ample light for intense leaf coloration.

   D. oerstedii: A smaller species with matte green leaves.

   D. oerstedii variegata: Leaves a dark green with a white midrib.

*German Ivy, *Senecio*
Moderately warm/Partial shade

A glossy, ivy-like leaf on a plant that trails or climbs. I keep my plant in a hanging glass ball, in an east window, where it requires occasional pinching to keep it from becoming

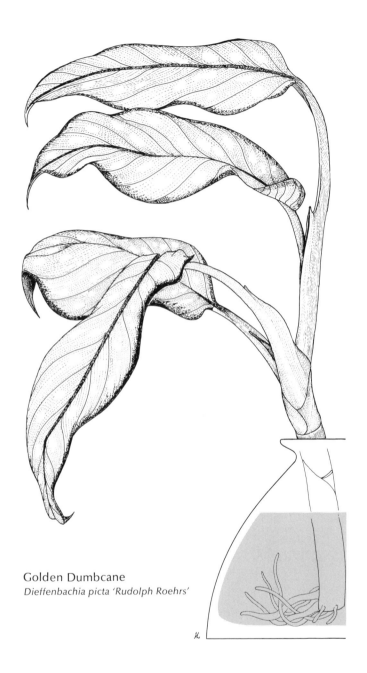

Golden Dumbcane
Dieffenbachia picta 'Rudolph Roehrs'

42

sparse looking. The full name is *Senecio mi-kanioides*. Many other members of the family are available. Why not experiment with a few?

Ivy, *Hedera*

Would you believe that there are more than 50 varieties of Ivy easily available to the house-plant enthusiast? Well, there are and then some. Many people collect Ivies only, and, when one is aware of the endless leaf varieties and colors, it's not surprising. Mine do quite well in plain water, as I plant them all outside for the summer and then take the best branches for winter cuttings, arranging them in a south window. They all look attractive when hanging over the edge of various bottles, or supported by a simple kind of trellis made of nylon fishing line strung on tacks. An old Chianti bottle hanging on nylon cord in my studio window is filled with Manda's Crested Ivy; on a bleak winter day, it's a cheery sight. Watch out for spider mites; Ivies particularly attract them.

H. canariensis variegata: Canary Islands Ivy. A beautiful leaf of slate-green, bluish green, and off-white with reddish stems. This Ivy will adapt to more warmth than the others.

H. helix: English Ivy. Apartment buildings like to landscape with this dark green Ivy, which does well under most ad-

43

Manda's
Crested Ivy

Hahn's
Selfbranching

Hedera helix

44

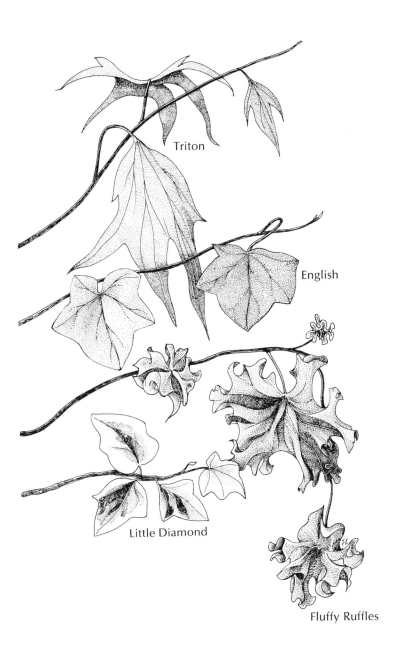

Triton

English

Little Diamond

Fluffy Ruffles

45

verse conditions and looks very cool on a hot summer day.

*H. helix 'Little Diamond': A lovely little Ivy with inch-long leaves mostly white and spotted with slate and bluish greens.

*H. helix 'Fluffy Ruffles': This Ivy is a baroque delight, with its curling ruffled edges, olive-green in color. The young leaves have reddish stems and are edged with a thick mass of short, brownish hairs that become less prominent as the leaf expands.

*H. helix 'Hahn's Selfbranching': A busy little Ivy that grows into a compact mass of stems and leaves.

*H. helix 'Manda's Crested': A star-shaped leaf of jade-green, with rosy edges that busily curl under and grow to about 3 inches.

*H. helix 'Triton': A beautiful light green leaf with three to seven long, waving fingers. My plant has a Japanese look as it trails over the edge of a chemical flask.

Hawaiian "Ti," Cordyline
Warm/Partial shade

Often called the "Good Luck Plant," the Hawaiian "Ti" in some places is sold as a small

"Lincoln Log" in a glassine or plastic envelope; you add water and it grows. The foliage of mature plants is used to make hula skirts and thatched roofs on the Islands. Supported by pebbles or gravel, in a low dish, it makes a most attractive plant.

*C. terminalis bicolor: Thin, green leaves edged with pink. Needs some sun to maintain the color.

  C. terminalis var. 'Ti': Spirally arranged, yellowish green leaf.

 C. terminalis 'Tricolor': Pink, red, and creamy-white leaves with a green background.

*Hawaiian Tree Fern, _Cibotium_
Warm/Partial shade

This is the kind of plant that, if everyone knew about it, everyone would have at least two. When placed against a plain wall, the plants create an instant jungle feeling, with 4-foot fronds waving in a gentle breeze. Light candles and serve planter's punch! Use a large enough container and plenty of stones to hold the plants erect. I've seen them grow to 30 feet in a Florida greenhouse, but you'll be content with the size they attain indoors. They are known under two names: C. chamissoi and C. meniziesii.

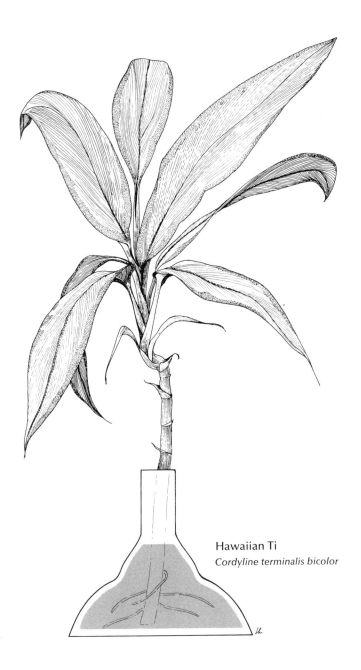

Hawaiian Ti
Cordyline terminalis bicolor

48

Hawaiian Tree Fern
Cibotium chamissoi

49

Japanese Spurge
Pachysandra terminalis

50

*Japanese Spurge, *Pachysandra*
Cool/Partial shade

Everyone in the city or suburbs knows this plant; it's used as a ground cover where nothing else will grow. It is an evergreen, 6 to 8 inches high, with glossy green leaves. Some time ago I was looking for more plants for the winter, pulled up some Pachysandra from the back yard, put it in water, and it has done beautifully. Since Pachysandra spreads fast as a ground cover, once it is established, even the stingiest suburban friend will be willing to give you some. On occasion it will flower with small greenish white blossoms. The full name is *P. terminalis.*

Miniature Sweet Flag, *Acorus*
Warm/Partial shade

This is a charming plant. It's also called the Japanese Sweet Flag, and one look will tell you why: it looks and is Japanese. I have had one in a cordial glass (which is a mistake in the long run, as the water dries out too fast and I have sometimes forgotten to add more) and new spring shoots had already started by mid-January.

A. gramineus pusillus: A dwarf form that barely exceeds 4 inches, with fresh, green, swordlike leaves.

**A. gramineus variegatus:* Swordlike leaves

Miniature Sweet Flag
Acorus gramineus variegatus

52

arranged in a fan with lengthwise stripes of white and green.

Miracle Plant, *Fatshedera*
Moderately warm/Partial shade

This durable and attractive plant is the result of an accidental cross between two plants: the Irish Ivy, *Hedera helix hibernica*, and a Japanese Aralia, *Fatsia japonica 'Moseri',* in a French greenhouse before World War I — a perfect example of the international scope of horticulture. The plant will tolerate very poor light and looks fine in a dark hall, but needs a summer session outdoors or on a patio to restore its vigor. The leaves can grow quite large (up to 8 inches in width), and it maintains a shrubby growth until it becomes top-heavy. If that happens, tie it up or trim it back.

F. lizei: Miracle Plant, Ivy Tree. This is the original hybrid and has dark green, shiny, five-lobed leaves.

*F. lizei variegata: Variegated Ivy Tree. Large green leaves mottled with lighter and darker shades of green edged with white.

Oleander, *Nerium*
Moderately warm/Sun

A beautiful evergreen shrub that is popular in the Deep South and Southwest.

53

Miracle Plant
Fatshedera lizei variegatus

54

It has beautiful blooms and dark green, sword-shaped, leathery leaves. Cuttings will readily root in water. In the north it is used as a pot or tub plant which is brought in for the winter. *Note that all parts of this plant are poisonous. N. oleander:* Rose-Bay. Rosy red flowers.

Philodendron   Warm/Partial shade

This is the stalwart family in house-plant lore—an amazing group of plants that can transform a drab bookcase, a dull bathroom, or a boring wall.

These are jungle plants that begin life on dark, moist, spongy ground formed of layers and layers of vegetable debris. As they grow, they climb the nearest supports, striving to reach light that continually filters through the tree branches above. The ground serves only as a holdfast and short-term feeding post, until the plants have sufficient anchorage to begin their climb. When allowed to trail from the edges of pots, the leaves remain rather small and sparse in growth, but let them proceed up the ladder and you'll be amazed at the change. When visiting the Fairchild Gardens in Miami, Florida, I saw Philodendrons of such magnificence that it was difficult to believe they belonged to the same family of plants as those found in variety stores, and hard to understand how many of the tree branches supported the weight of these lush vines.

In an east window of my studio, three Philodendrons (Burgundy, Fiddle-leaf, Cut-leaved) sit in glass jars made from quart beer bottles, suspended by nylon fishing line (see page 91), their stems supported by lucite rods. The aerial roots branch out in all directions, and the plants sway whenever someone walks by. The temperature is warm, and the light is dimmed, after 11 a.m., by trees outside, so that the plants are as close to their natural habitat as I can get. As most of the fertilizer received by these plants in the wild comes from rain water trickling down tree trunks, absorbing insect and animal wastes on the way, and in turn being absorbed by the aerial roots of the Philodendrons, I fertilize them in much the same way by spraying the leaves and stems about once every two weeks with a solution of very weak plant food, using a hand mister. The plants are misted with warm water to simulate jungle humidity, and the leaves are cleansed of their dust accumulation about once a month. Their roots sit in plain water, and the plants thrive.

Philodendrons are divided into two groups: the *climbers*, which eventually need some type of support to grow on, and the *self-headers*, which send out their leaves from a common point and eventually the stem becomes a trunk.

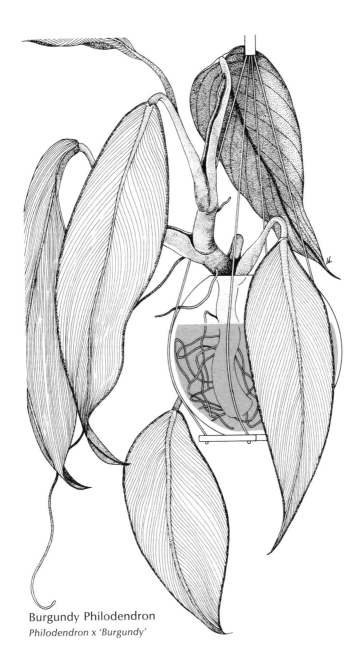

Burgundy Philodendron
Philodendron x 'Burgundy'

57

*P. × 'Burgundy': Burgundy Philodendron. A compact climber with leathery leaves up to a foot long, shaped like an arrow as they mature; color is deep green, with a red-wine cast and red stems.

P. cannifolium: Flask Philodendron. Self-header with spear-shaped leaves and continually swollen stems.

P. domesticum: Elephant's Ear. Good climber and very tropical looking. Green, arrow shaped leaves that resemble elongated hearts.

*P. oxycardium: Heartleaf Philodendron. Also called P. cordatum. Probably the most well-known plant in America. If nothing else ever succeeded in a home, the Heartleaf could be depended on. Put it on a bare shelf in the worst light imaginable and it will exist, although the leaves will become very small; but give it a support and some light and you'll be surprised by the change.

*P. panduraeforme: Fiddle-leaf Philodendron. A very good climber with a leaf that resembles the head of a fiddle.

*P. radiatum: Cut-leaved Philodendron. Also called P. dubium because the plant collectors originally were not sure about its identification. A good climber, with light green leaves and stems.

58

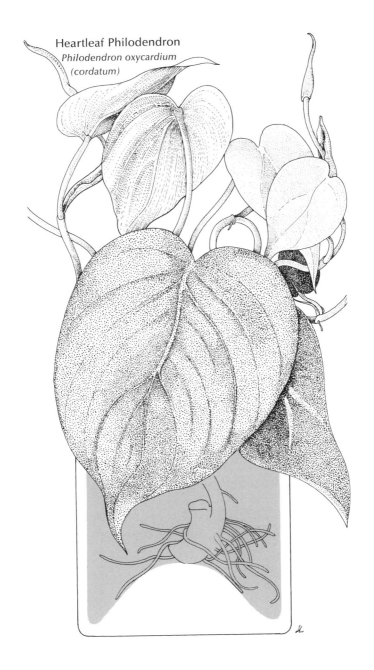

Heartleaf Philodendron
Philodendron oxycardium
(cordatum)

59

Fiddle-leaf Philodendron (juvenile)
Philodendron panduraeforme

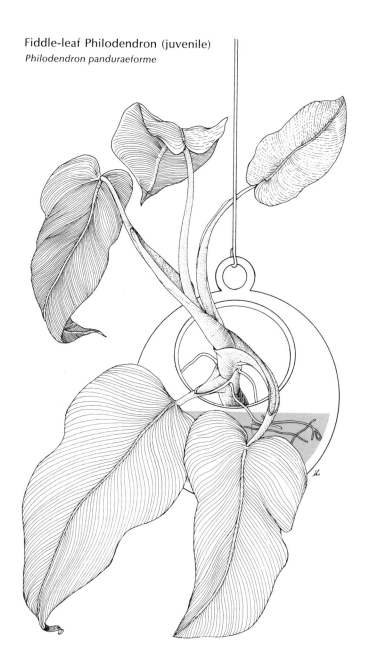

60

Cut-leaved Philodendron

Philodendron radiatum
(dubium)

61

Silver-leaf Philodendron
(juvenile form)
Philodendron sodiroi

62

P. sodiroi: Silver-leaf Philodendron. The
leaves are a bluish green, with an over-
all cast of silver. The plant is a climber,
and the leaves change in shape as the
plant matures. At the present writing,
mine is a young plant, and, because
I've found no pictures of a mature leaf,
I've no idea how they change.

P. *wendlandii:* Bird's Nest Philodendron. A
self-header with waxy green leaves and
a pronounced midrib. The membrane
covering developing leaves is white.

*Piggy-back Plant, *Tolmiea*
Moderately warm/Partial shade

A charming little plant with light, fresh
green leaves, basically heart-shaped, with cut
edges and covered with small hairs. New
plants arise at the base of the leaf, perfect but
miniature imitations of the parent. In poor
light the stems become rather long and arching, but in good light the plant becomes much
more bushy and compact. Every one of the
little plantlets will root, and, I imagine, if one
keeps it up, the country could be overrun! Use
a nutrient solution. The full name is *T.
menziesii.*

Pothos, *Scindapsus*   Warm/Partial shade

A happy vine that has one fault: it

Piggy-back Plant
Tolmiea menziesii

64

needs warmth and, unless it gets it, does absolutely nothing. Pothos are fine for the edges of tables or bookshelves, or for being hung against walls. Reasonably good light is required to keep the color, but it's worth the extra effort. In tropical climates, the leaves become quite large, but here (northeastern United States) be contented if they reach 5 inches. The vine creeps and trails or will climb if given support.

S. *aureus*: Devil's Ivy. Often called Golden Pothos. Broad, dark green leaves blotched with yellow and having a very waxy look. Pinch them back if you get tired of the length.

S. *aureus 'Marble Queen'*: A variety with many streaks of pure white through the leaves.

S. *aureus 'Tricolor'*: Having the same leaf as the others, but the basic green is dappled with yellow, yellowish green, and creamy-white.

*S. *pictus argyraeus*: Satin Pothos. A beautiful leaf with a satin-like finish over a bluish green background completely edged with silver, and with random silver markings on the surface.

Spiderworts, *Tradescantia*
Moderately warm/Partial shade

These attractively colored little creep-

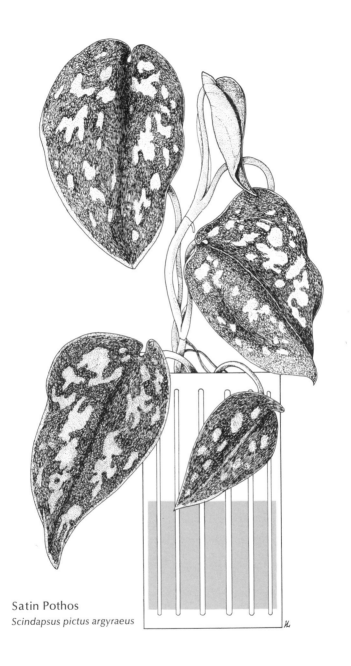

Satin Pothos
Scindapsus pictus argyraeus

66

ers belong to the same genus as the popular garden flower Virginia Spiderwort. Their respective flowers are almost identical except for size and color. The blossoms last one day. Also called Inch Plants because, with their speedy growth, they "inch along," and Wandering Jew as they closely resemble the Mexican *Zebrina pendula* which is also known as Wandering Jew (see below). Confusing? Not really, as they all belong to the same family. They are very good for hanging over the edges of jars or creeping along shelves. The bright color of the leaves will slowly fade if they are not exposed to enough light. These creepers have a tendency to become quite rampant in growth, so pinch them back if necessary. Although many will grow quite well in plain water, I generally add some nutrient.

T. blossfeldiana: Flowering Inch Plant. Olive-green leaves with purple under sides and stems; covered with silvery hairs. The Flowering Inch Plant blossoms quite freely with pale purple flowers.

T. fluminensis: Wandering Jew. Shiny green leaves, purple beneath, on twisting stems. The flower is white.

T. fluminensis 'Variegata': Variegated Wandering Jew. Green leaves with bands of yellow and creamy-white. White flowers.

Swedish Ivy, *Plectranthus*

Warm/Partial shade

A hardy plant for hanging pots, because their soft stems bend quite easily. The plants have rounded, scalloped leaves of dark green on both upper and under sides, with brownish stems. They are not spectacular, but they are reliable.

P. *australis*: Swedish Ivy.

*P. *coleoides* 'Marginatus'*: White-edged
    Swedish Ivy.

Sweet Potato, *Ipomoea*

Moderately warm/Sun

This is a special favorite of mine as it wings the mind back to grade school and basic botany when everyone grew sweet-potato vines in the sunniest window. There was such excitement when the first roots crept out, and by the time five or six shoots had appeared at the top and the class voted for the best four, teachers had to rap for silence. Well, it's still an exciting plant to grow and one can become quite inventive when trying to outdo the old toothpick approach. Remember the old instructions? Take a Mason jar half full of water and suspend the potato on four or five toothpicks thrust into the sides so that the bottom of the potato just touches the water. Replace the water as it evaporates. The old way still works but, with all the attractive plastics and new containers available today, try to improvise a bit.

When on a drive in the country, buy your potato in a small grocery store. If the tuber is bought in the city, check it for signs of life, as many of these vegetables are dried for market and will not sprout. I've read that the fat part of the tuber goes up. It's always been the reverse for me, so try both ends. The roots are white and the shoots purple-green.

Incidentally, while on the subject of vegetables, don't forget carrot tops. Cut off the top 2 inches of a fairly fresh carrot and place it in a dish on wet gravel or pebbles so the cut carrot just touches the water. Don't submerge any part of the carrot or it will rot.

Or why not try the pineapple? Get one with a top that is not battered and bruised. Cut off the top, leaving at least 2 inches of the fruit, and scrape out the pulpy center; then set it on wet gravel or pebbles.

Beets should work in this way too, but I've never tried them; a cut beet will "bleed."

These may not sound very sophisticated, but the splashes of green can be very refreshing here and there in your windows.

Umbrella Plant, *Cyperus*

Warm/Partial shade

The Umbrella Plants conjure up visions

of one's floating down broad rivers into sunsets streaked with gold and passing Pyramids on the left. No wonder, as one of the family is the Papyrus used in Egypt for making papyrus paper 3000 years before Christ. A grouping of Umbrella Plants in water in an old battery jar makes a welcome sight, and some, with proper care, grow quite large and are very imposing.

Occasionally the tips of the leaves turn brown, and I've been told, and also have read, that the pH of the water, if too acid, affects the plant. The water should have a neutral pH (pH 7). If you have a well, the acidity may fluctuate with the seasons. A pH measuring device is very inexpensive at any garden center, or perhaps the corner druggist will donate some litmus paper. At any rate, if you have hard water (you always get a ring around the tub when using soap) boil it before using it for these plants. See page 16 above for testing the alkalinity or acidity of the water you use and the means of getting a neutral pH.

C. alternifolius: Umbrella Plant. Ribbed stems of bright, grassy green, topped with a rosette of grasslike leaves much like the spokes of an umbrella. In the spring brownish green flowers grow above the crown of the leaves.

C. alternifolius gracilis: Dwarf Umbrella Plant is just what the name implies; it grows only about 1 foot high.

Umbrella Plant
Cyperus diffusus

C. diffusus: More squat and bushy in appearance than the others in the genus. The stem is triangular, and the leaves are quite broad, with a rough edge that you can feel by running your finger along the edge toward the stem.

C. *diffusus variegatus:* Striped Umbrella Palm. The leaves are striped with pale yellow and cream color.

*Umbrella Tree, *Brassaia*

Warm/Partial shade

Large Umbrella Trees are seen in the lobbies of some banks and insurance companies; they can grow quite large with a minimum of care. They are one of those plants that adapt to almost any light conditions as long as the air is warm. My plant was started as a seedling given to me by a friend. I put it in a glass of water, where it has been for more than a year and, although not growing terribly fast, it is quite healthy. The full name is *B. actinophylla,* and the plant is sometimes called *Schefflera actinophylla.*

Wandering Jew, *Zebrina*

Moderately warm/Sun

Creeping vines that have been popular house plants for years. They resemble the Spiderworts (except for technical botanical

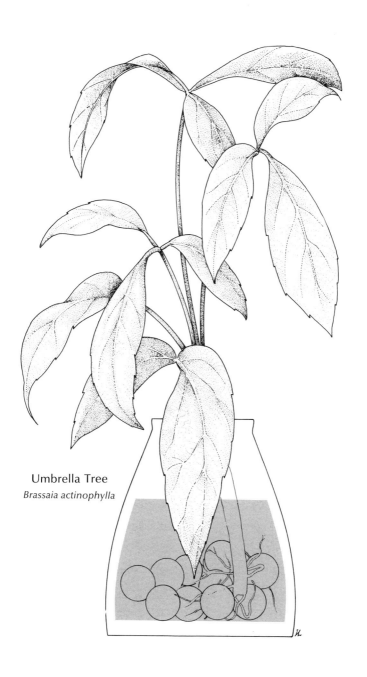

Umbrella Tree
Brassaia actinophylla

73

Variegated Wandering Jew
Zebrina pendula 'Discolor'

74

differences). These plants are fast and rampant growers and will need to be pinched back occasionally. They bloom with small, three-petaled flowers that last only a day.

Z. *pendula:* Silvery Wandering Jew. Deep green and purple leaves with two silver bands.

*Z. *pendula* 'Discolor':* Variegated Wandering Jew. Reddish brown leaves with purple and silver stripes.

Z. *pendula* 'Quadricolor':* Gay Wandering Jew. This leaf is a beauty. Purple-green leaves banded with white and shaded with pink and red.

Z. *purpusii:* Bronze Wandering Jew. Fleshy and broad leaves that make a wonderful display hanging from a wall container. With good light the shiny green tops of the leaves contrast sharply with the under sides which become a very dark purple.

Others to Try

Many more plants than those mentioned above will remain fresh in water or even take root. Pussy willows will leaf out after the catkins, or flowers, have bloomed. Weeping-willow stems will root and put out buds and shoots. Periwinkle, or myrtle, makes a most attractive arching fountain of leaves, and roots will form on many of the stems.

Start these in the spring. Another springtime water lover, of course, is Forsythia. Geraniums and Impatiens are common garden flowers that find themselves at home in a glass.

A host of grasses from marshy and swampy areas will last a season in the house. Water Chestnuts *(Trapa natans)*, Water-Fern *(Ceratopteris thalictroides)*, and Parrot's Feather *(Myriophyllum proserpinacoides)* are fresh and exciting in bowls of water.

How about an under-water garden? The Amazon Sword Plant *(Echinodorus brevipedi-cellatus)*, Cape Fear Spatterdock *(Nuphar sagittifolia)*, or the common Eel Grass *(Vallis-neria torta)* are all common under-water plants that can be found at aquarium and pet stores. They require very little care except for removal of leaves that have turned brown and an adjustment of light conditions (no direct sun). While looking for these, search out the Madagascar Lace Plant or Laceleaf *(Apono-geton fenestralis)*, a large and very beautiful submerged plant with leaves resembling crochet or macramé embroidery. Do not put it in direct sun, use soft water (below pH 7), and never let the temperature go below 65° F. Planted with gravel in a cylinder of glass and with the right backlighting, it becomes an art object. The leaves may attain a foot in length, but remember to keep the water clean.

Keep looking and you'll find more!

chapter 4 · BULBS IN WATER

When the cold winds of winter sweep through the streets of northern cities and snow piles up to kitchen-window ledges out in the country; when you're drenched with the sleet and icy rains while trudging to the mailbox or corner delicatessen and returning home with a burning hate for nature, nothing is quite so lovely and encouraging to the spirit as the sight of spring flowers glowing in a water-filled container on a windowsill or coffee table.

Years ago it was a common practice to "force" spring bulbs for Christmas flowers, and much cheaper than going to a florist. It's still more economical and much easier than most people think. While a rich soil will produce a more showy flower, it's not necessary; the flower is already formed, small and perfect, covered by the leaf layers of the bulb. "Forcing" is a rather unpleasant name for the process. All you are doing is speeding up the timetable of the seasons, making the bulb think that December or January is March or April, when it is returned to the warmth of a room.

Two types of bulbs are available: the hardy, outdoor types such as Hyacinth, Crocus, and Lily-of-the-Valley (technically not a bulb but a rootstock called a "pip") and the "tender" bulbs that will not survive a northern winter. The latter are the Paper-white Narcissus, the Soleil d'Or, and the Chinese Sacred Lilies.

These bulbs can all be found in fall garden catalogues or in garden supply stores, where part of the preparations for winter blooming have already been done for you by the nurseries: the bulbs have been preconditioned to bloom early by controlled fluctuations in temperatures. A word of caution: never let any of these bulbs dry out once you've started their growth, for they will not survive such treatment.

Hyacinths, *Hyacinthus*

French Roman Hyacinths bloom a bit earlier than the common hyacinth, and have fewer flowers but make up for it with their intense fragrance. Any glass container with sufficient area for root development and a neck that is narrower than the width of the bulb will do. I grow my bulbs in small, gradu-

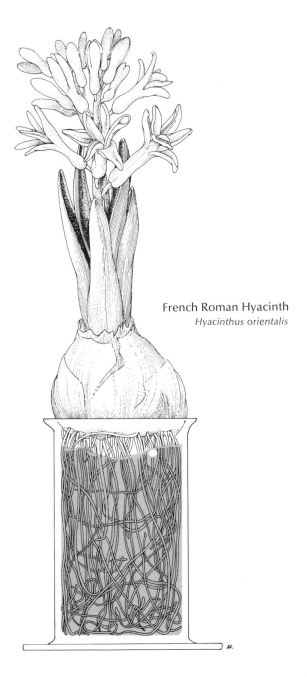

French Roman Hyacinth
Hyacinthus orientalis

79

ated cylinders (see illustration) so that the pattern of the roots becomes as interesting as the plants.

In forcing, the bulbs must be made to believe that a period of winter has already passed. I use the refrigerator for this deception. Fill the container with water so that it just touches the bottom of the bulb (no higher or the bulb may rot) and set it in the rear shelf of the refrigerator, perhaps on a piece of cardboard or the like to prevent accidental tipping when the door is slammed. Leave the bulbs for about a month, checking to see that the water level is kept up and watch for the roots to develop. The bulb must never be allowed to send up leaves or buds without sufficient roots or they will not bloom.

When the white, twining roots have filled the glass container, remove it and place it in a cool, shady area for about five days. Then you can bring it to a cool, sunny window, rotating the container daily so the flower stalks remain straight as they grow and don't begin to lean in one direction.

I start mine about the first of November and have blooms for Christmas and New Year's. By staggering your schedule, flowers may be had for most of the winter. When storing these bulbs for later use, keep them in paper or plastic bags with holes punched to allow air circulation, in the bottom of the refrigerator and make sure they do not become damp or wet during this dormancy or they may spoil.

Hyacinths come in many beautiful colors: L'Innocence: Pure White; City of Haarlem: Yellow; Jan Bos: Bright Red; Perle Brilliant: Light Blue; Pink Pearl: Delft Blue.

Hyacinth glasses were once found in most households. Today, the old ones have become antiques, but new glasses are offered in many garden catalogues and, recently, plastic containers have appeared on the market. They are shaped much like an hourglass, the upper segment holding the bulb just above the water level, or have a plastic frame with projections to hold the bulb. The procedures are the same as for the French Roman Hyacinth, but these varieties take longer to mature, usually three months from start to bloom.

Remove the glass from the refrigerator when the jar is filled with roots and the top shoot is about two inches high. Put it in a cool area with an inverted paper cone over the top for about two weeks to prevent the buds from blooming before the stem is long enough. After the flowering has commenced, try to keep the plants in a cool spot so the flowers will last longer.

Unfortunately, these bulbs are completely depleted by forcing, and must be discarded after they have once bloomed.

81

Lily-of-the-Valley
Convallaria majalis

82

Lily-of-the-Valley, *Convallaria*

These are available at the same time as the other bulbs and usually come pre-planted in a special mix to which you just add water. You can, however, save a bit of money by buying the pips and planting them yourself. They can be potted in almost any material that will hold moisture, even sand, but I use aquarium gravel in bowls or dishes at least 3 inches high. The pips are placed in the gravel or sand with the buds just above the surface, watered thoroughly, and placed in a cardboard box (with holes punched in the sides for ventilation) for about two weeks at room temperature. Then place them in a darkened area of the room for a few days before exposing the plants to bright light.

Crocus

The familiar blues and yellows of Crocus of early spring are easily grown for indoor bloom. Use a container that is deep enough to allow the roots to develop without pushing the bulbs out of the gravel; fill with gravel or sand and set at least six bulbs (for a showy display) on the top so that bulbs will always be out of the water. Fill with water, and follow the refrigerator routine. If you use a glass container, the development of the roots is quite fascinating. Always remember to keep

Yellow Crocus
Crocus moesicus

84

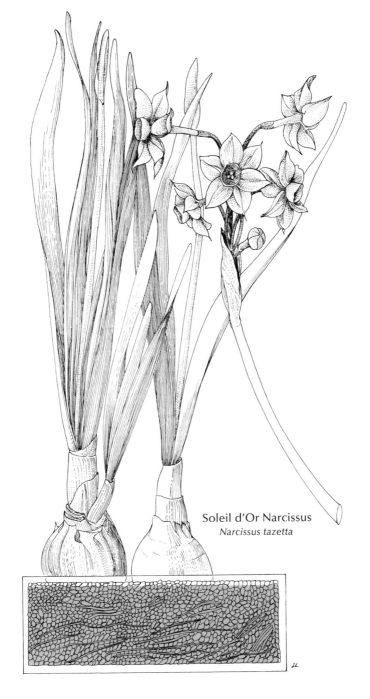

Soleil d'Or Narcissus
Narcissus tazetta

85

the bulbs in darkness until active root growth is evident, or they will not flower. Crocuses can also be grown in a small glass, like hyacinths, but are not really showy enough to warrant it.

Narcissus

For Paper-white Narcissus, Soleil d'Or, and Chinese Sacred Lilies choose containers that are deep enough for root development. Fill two-thirds full with gravel and add water to the top of the gravel. Then place the bulbs on top of the gravel, gently, and surround the bulbs with more gravel to keep them upright, leaving the top half clear. Since these bulbs come from gentler climates and are once again specially preconditioned by the growers, they do not require intense cold to start them off. Place them in a cool (50°-60°), dark, well-ventilated spot until the shoots are about 3 inches tall. Move the pot to a lighted area (a north window is perfect) for three or four days, then set the pot in the sun. Rotate the container occasionally so that the leaves do not lean. Always keep the gravel moist, but never let the bulbs themselves get wet, only their roots. When my bulbs were planted at the first of November, the Soleil d'Or bloomed the week before Christmas, the Paper Whites between Christmas and New Year's, and the Chinese Sacred Lilies the third week of January.

chapter 5 · ALL ABOUT CONTAINERS

Thousands of common-place and not-so-common-place objects can make exciting containers for your plants: old medicine bottles, green wine jars, and antique milk bottles—to name only a few. In the previous section I have tried to indicate some of the possibilities by drawing each plant in a different shape of container.

You will soon go way beyond these suggestions. An amazing amount of the accumulation of years (upper shelves of a kitchen cupboard; dusty corner of an old attic) can be dragged out and rethought with an idea toward water-plant display. Every time I sit down to think of possible containers, I usually come up with several fresh ideas. What follows are some general areas of container exploration that I have found fruitful.

Chemical Glassware: For many years, shapes and forms of glass have been developed for use in chemical laboratories that embody the principles of modern design. Since the chemist has no time to be bothered with superfluous appendages, appliques, and gee-gaws (can you imagine a Victorian test tube?), most types of chemical glassware hold their own with contemporary bowls, vases, jars, and stemware produced by the design leaders of today. In addition, most of it is made of heat-resistant glass. Since much of it is available at chemical supply houses, and can easily be purchased by the layman, descriptions of the basic shapes are given below with a clue to an understanding of the metric system (most of this glassware is measured in milliliters).

• *Battery Jars:* Straight-sided cylinders of clear glass available in pints, quarts, and gallons. A 1-gallon jar is about 8 inches high and 6 inches in diameter.

• *Beakers:* Clear glass jars with a lip for pouring. They are in various capacities measured in milliliters. Just remember that 30 milliliters approximately equal 1 ounce. One liter is approximately 1 quart.

• *Bottles:* Straight-sided with narrow mouth, wide mouth or extra-wide mouth; usually measured in ounces.

• *Flasks:* They are clear glass and come in two basic shapes: Florence and Erlenmeyer. They are measured in milliliters. A 250-milli-

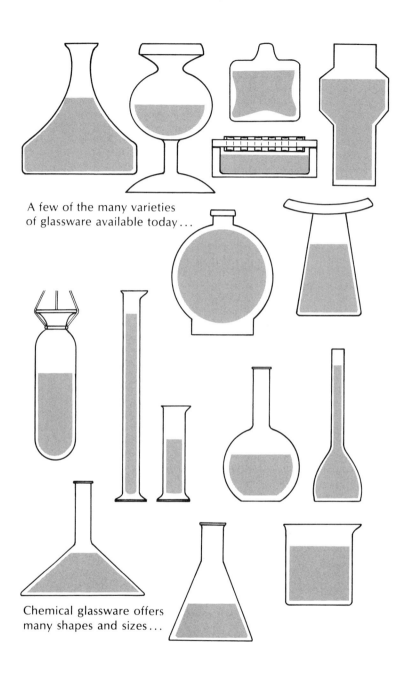

A few of the many varieties
of glassware available today...

Chemical glassware offers
many shapes and sizes...

89

liter Erlenmeyer flask is about 5 inches high and 2½ inches wide at the bottom, narrowing to 1½ inches at the top.

• *Graduated Cylinders:* These are used to measure liquids and are marked in milliliters. Cylinders are also available without the measuring lines etched in the glass and are called, naturally, ungraduated cylinders.

• *Museum Jars:* Tall cylinders of glass made for display or the storage of specimens. They are measured in inches; a typical size is 1 foot high and 2 inches in diameter.

• *Show Bottles:* Round-bottomed bottles with pinched-in necks, topped with a cork. They are usually filled with mineral specimens and stood on their corks. Remove the cork, tie nylon fishing line around the neck, and they make great hanging jars.

• *Volumetric Flasks:* These have a round bottom, with just enough flat area to stand properly, and a very tall neck. They're measured in milliliters and serve as good-looking bud vases.

• *Test Tubes:* Test-tube racks are still often made of wood and hold six or twelve tubes. Put an ivy cutting in each test tube and you will have a fine display.

Bottle Cutters: In the last few years, a number of different varieties of home bottle cutters have been marketed; the manufacturers even sponsor late movies on television.

I have been pleasantly surprised to find that, when the directions are followed properly, these devices really work, and many wine bottles can be turned into colored glassware that is economic, pleasing in looks, and help-ful by not being thrown out to clutter the en-vironment. Mayonnaise bottles, pickle bot-tles, and the like work perfectly as containers when their tops are severed. Depending on your free time and the amount of epoxy in the house, structures can be made that will reach the ceiling. Speaking of wine bottles, rip the raffia off a Chianti bottle, and you will be surprised to see that some now have flat bottoms.

Hanging Gardens: Many variety and department stores carry small acrylic squares, strung with nylon fishing line that will hold almost any shape of container up to 25 pounds in weight. Consider these for a hanging bottle garden with plants at various heights in front of a window or serving as a room divider.

You can make your own quite easily and support even more weight by using nylon cord or a fishing line of heavier test. Just drill a small hole in each corner of a piece of acrylic or plywood for a base. Then cut two pieces of cord the same length. Pass each cord through two of the holes (diagonally if you care to) and gather the ends. Slip a glass or plastic bead on the cords for tension and tie

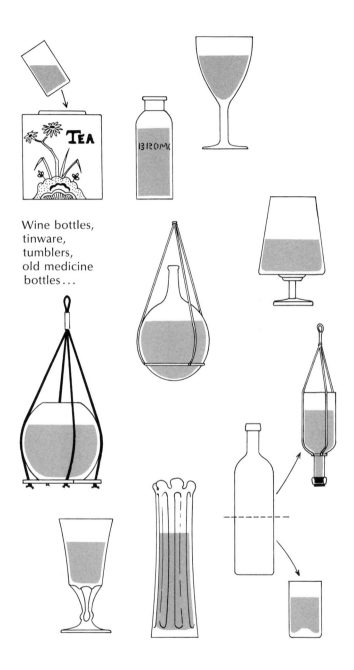

Wine bottles,
tinware,
tumblers,
old medicine
bottles...

92

them to a cafe-curtain ring. Vary the length of the cords, and you vary the heights of the bottles.

Vases: Since the country has become more ecologically minded, the number of bud vases and flower holders based on clever and valid design principles has rapidly increased. This past year, I've seen glass balls that hold flowers (or plants) combined with candles; bud vases made with twenty to thirty hollow glass rods bound together in cylinder form; clear glass marbles wrapped in nylon fishnet for plant-holding "frogs"; bent-glass tubing in many shapes and sizes; clear and colored acrylic flower pots; and many more variations on the old standbys. Most of them are stunning when combined with the right plants in a water garden.

But don't forget those old cracked heirlooms. When small glasses are used as waterproof liners, even tin tea canisters take on a new look and function. Concrete drain pipes and tiles can be stood on end and lined with a plastic or glass bottle to fill a corner with cascades of green. An old glass kerosene-lamp base, when properly washed and filled with a few trailers, takes on a new look. Old Mason jars, electrical insulators, glasses from the supermarket, and even the old glass brick of the thirties start life anew when used with plants.

SOURCES OF SUPPLY

Most of the equipment required, including plants in many cases, can now be found at variety stores, and many department stores also carry plants, containers, and various supplies for the water gardener. In addition, a number of reputable firms ship plants by mail.

Chemical Glassware

Carolina Biological Supply Company
Burlington, North Carolina 27215

Edmund Scientific Co.
605 Edscorp Building
Barrington, New Jersey 08007

Ward's Natural Science Establishment
3000 East Ridge Road
Rochester, New York 14622

Welch Scientific Company
7300 North Linder Avenue
Skokie, Illinois 60076

Plastics

AIN Plastics, Inc.
65 Fourth Avenue
New York, New York 10003

94

Bulbs

P. de Jager & Sons, Inc.
188 Ashbury Street
South Hamilton, Massachusetts 01982

Van Bourgondien's
245 Farmingdale Road, Route 109
Box A, Babylon, New York 11702

Plants

W. Atlee Burpee Co.
Philadelphia, Pennsylvania 19132

Edelweiss Gardens
54 Robbinsville-Allentown Road
Robbinsville, New Jersey 08691

The House Plant Corner
P. O. Box 810
Oxford, Maryland 21654

Logee's Greenhouses
Danielson, Connecticut 06239

Loyce's Flowers
Route 2
Granbury, Texas 76048

Merry Gardens
Camden, Maine 04843

Norvell Greenhouses
318 South Greenacres Road
Greenacres, Washington 99016

George W. Park Seed Co., Inc.
Greenwood, South Carolina 29646

INDEX

Arrowheads *(Syngonium)*, 24-27
  African Evergreen, **25,** 27
  Arrowhead Plant, **26,** 27
Bloodleaf *(Iresine)*, **28,** 29
  Yellow Bloodleaf, **28,** 29
Cactus, 22
Charcoal, use as purifier, 19
Chinese Evergreens
  (Aglaonema), 19, 29-31
  Pewter Chinese Evergreen,
    30, 31
  Ribbon Plant, **8**
Cleaning plants, instruction for,
  20-21
Coleus (Painted Nettle), 31-34
  Coleus blumei 'Brilliancy,'
    32, **33**
Containers, 13, 87-93
Crocus, 83, 84, 86
Dracaena, 19, 34-40
  Gold-dust Dracaena, **8,** 36, **37**
  Madagascar Dragon Tree, 26, **38**
  Ribbon Plant, **8,** 34, 36, **39,** 40
  Striped Dracaena, 34, **35**
Dumbcanes *(Dieffenbachia)*,
  40-42
  Golden Dumbcane, 41, **42**
"Forcing," 77, 78, 80-81
German Ivy *(Senecio)*, 41-42
Hawaiian "Ti" *(Cordyline)*, 46-48
Hawaiian Tree Fern
  (Cibotium), 47, **49**
Holdfasts, 14-15
Hyacinths *(Hyacinthus)*, 78-81
  French Roman Hyacinth, 78, **79**
Hydroculture, 9
Hydroponics, 9
Insects, elimination of, 21
Ivy *(Hedera)*, 19, 43-47
  Diamond Ivy, **45,** 46
  English Ivy, 43-44, **45**
  Fluffy Ruffles Ivy, **45,** 46
  Hahn's Selfbranching Ivy, **44,** 46
  Manda's Crested Ivy, **44,** 46
  Triton Ivy, **45,** 46

Japanese Spurge
  (Pachysandra), **50,** 51
Light, 23
Lily-of-the-Valley
  (Convallaria), **82,** 83
Miniature Sweet Flag
  (Acorus), 51, **52,** 53
Miracle Plant *(Fatshedera)*, 53, 54
  Variegated Ivy Tree, **54**
Narcissus, **85,** 86
  Soleil d'Or, **85,** 86
Nephthytis, 27
Oleander *(Nerium)*, 53, 55
Painted Nettle *(Coleus)*, 31-34, **33**
Philodendron, 55-63
  Burgundy Philodendron,
    56, **57,** 58
  Cut-leaved Philodendron,
    56, 58, **61**
  Fiddle-leaf Philodendron,
    56, 58, **60**
  Heartleaf Philodendron, 58, **59**
  Silver-leaf Philodendron, **62,** 63
Piggy-back Plant *(Tolmiea)*, 63, **64**
Plant food, 17-18
Pothos *(Scindapsus)*, 63, 65, 66
  Satin pothos, 65, **66**
Spiderworts *(Tradescantia)*, 65, 67
Swedish Ivy *(Plectranthus)*, 68
Sweet Potato *(Ipomoea)*, 68
Temperature, 23
Umbrella Plant *(Cyperus)*, 8, 19,
  69-72, **71**
Umbrella Tree *(Brassaia)*, 19, 72, **73**
Wandering Jew *(Zebrina)*, **8,** 72,
  74, 75
  Variegated, **74**
Water, 15
  acidity, 15, 16
  changing of, 19, 20
  chlorine level, 16
  rain water, 17
Woodward, John, 9